The Journey of the Beatitudes

About the book:
The author shares his interpretation of the Beatitudes as a plan for living an abundant life. The eight opening statements from Jesus' Sermon on the Mount are examined as teaching statements, followed by promises to us for living the way these statements suggest. The Beatitudes are explored as a Christian process, similar to the Twelve Step process for recovering people in Alcoholics Anonymous. The author believes the central message in each process is essentially the same.

About the author:
Richard Wilson has been the creative director of a Minneapolis advertising firm for many years. His avocation is writing musicals, many of which are on religious subjects. He has had three record albums of Christian songs produced. This is his first published book.

The Journey of the Beatitudes

RICHARD WILSON

First published July, 1986.

ISBN: 0-89486-363-0

Printed in the United States of America.

Editor's Note:
  Hazelden Educational Materials offers a variety of information on chemical dependency and related areas. Our
publications do not necessarily represent Hazelden or its
programs, nor do they officially speak for any Twelve Step
organization.

INTRODUCTION

This book is about an idea. The Beatitudes, the eight opening statements Jesus spoke in His Sermon on the Mount, are a step-by-step guide to how we should live, and their message closely resembles the message in the Twelve Steps of Alcoholics Anonymous.

The ideas are to use in your meditation and life planning. We will explore the meaning of the words Jesus spoke, see how each beatitude leads to the next, and learn how this is related to the program of A.A.

The Twelve Steps of Alcoholics Anonymous are a step-by-step process created to help alcoholics find their way from the insanity of alcoholism to the serenity and sanity of a life controlled by a Higher Power and personal honesty. This Twelve Step program has been adopted by other groups because it works so well in our dealings with almost any controlling and harmful influence in our lives.

A few years ago, I began to wonder why there wasn't a similar, systematic approach to the teachings of Jesus. I saw confusion about the real way of life Jesus proposed. What was morally right? What was being "born again"? What was faith? What were good works? Which of these was most important? These were some of the questions I heard asked by young people and others flirting with stronger faith.

I began to look through the Bible for something similar to the Twelve Steps. I found what I was looking for in the Beatitudes, the opening lines to the Sermon on the Mount, Matthew 5. Each begins with the word *blessed*. Jesus connects eight subjects together beginning with "Blessed are the poor in spirit, for theirs is the kingdom of heaven."

The more I looked at these, the more I saw a connection and progression. It was an eight-step process Jesus gave us as a way to follow Him. The Beatitudes were a journey.

Let us start at the beginning. If you decided to read the New Testament beginning with the book of Matthew, you would first learn about the lineage of the family of Abraham, David, and Jesus, and how they're connected. Following this is a short synopsis of Jesus' birth, the escape of Mary, Joseph, and Jesus to Egypt and when it was safe, their move back to Nazareth. Next comes John the Baptist preaching in the wilderness, telling the people to repent because the kingdom of heaven was at hand. You then read of Jesus' baptism and His temptations in the wilderness. Hearing of the imprisonment of John the Baptist, Jesus came back to the shores of the Sea of Galilee to begin His ministry.

The Book of Matthew tells us that Jesus lived in a town on the north shore of Galilee called Capernaum. Jesus gathered up some of His disciples and "taught and healed all manner of sickness" and, because of this healing, many people followed Him. He drew crowds, and to these followers He gave His Sermon on the Mount. It begins with a preamble we call the Beatitudes.

Because the word "blessed" is repeated nine times by Jesus, some people think there are nine beatitudes. Others think there are eight. I believe there are eight for two reasons. The "ninth" beatitude is a reinterpretation of the eighth and makes a transition into the rest of the Sermon on the Mount. I also think of the Beatitudes as having the symmetry and perfection of a poem or a song, usually written in sections of four or eight lines.

I like to think of the Beatitudes as a poem of Jesus. In a fine poem there is usually deep meaning. The Beatitudes, along with their rhythm and symmetry, have a feeling of wholeness, like a poem.

Moses originally brought the Ten Commandments to the people of God. The Beatitudes are the new commandments Jesus brings us. These new commandments relate to the grace of God rather than the laws of God. These Beatitudes are similar to the Ten Commandments. Each message shows us the way of life God means for us to live. The Beatitudes differ from the Ten Commandments because each beatitude contains a teaching statement about a way to live and gives us a promise for living that way.

The Beatitudes are a journey. Journeys are made up of the *passage* from a certain location to arrival at a *destination*. Like a journey, each beatitude is made up of the passage along the way, and the destination, or the promise. Each beatitude leads to the next, flowing along one step at a time. The messages are not meant for "know-it-alls"; they are meant for those who want to learn how to travel through life.

My hope is that, as you learn the meanings in each beatitude, you will see how rich they are in good sense and how important they can be to your life. For me the Beatitudes used to be nice words, but they weren't meaningful. They have become real and helpful in my day to day living. I hope they can become meaningful for you.

THE BEATITUDES

Blessed are the poor in spirit, for theirs is the kingdom of heaven.

Blessed are they that mourn, for they shall be comforted.

Blessed are the meek, for they shall inherit the earth.

Blessed are they which do hunger and thirst after righteousness, for they shall be filled.

Blessed are the merciful, for they shall obtain mercy.

Blessed are the pure in heart, for they shall see God.

Blessed are the peacemakers, for they shall be called the children of God.

Blessed are they which are persecuted for righteousness' sake, for theirs is the kingdom of heaven.

1

. . . to relate to God through our powerlessness

The Headline of The Bible

The first beatitude, "Blessed are the poor in spirit, for theirs is the kingdom of heaven," has been called "The Headline of the Bible," because it is the fundamental message, the first step. Unless we take this first step and accept our poverty of spirit, it will be *impossible* for us to follow Jesus. This step may seem rather sorrowful, but it is simply the necessary truth.

In the story of Adam and Eve, God had one very important thing to say to them, "Thou shall not eat of the tree of knowledge of good and evil." It was the forbidden fruit. God was really saying to Adam and Eve that things would be *good*, if they realized that *God* had all knowledge. They would desire God's knowledge, but they should surrender this desire to "be God."

Jesus says a similar thing to us in the first beatitude. If our lives are to be good, we must let God do His own work. We are poor in God's power and knowledge. Another word for this is *spirit*. God is rich in spirit; we are poor. We need to understand and accept this powerlessness to truly relate to God.

The first beatitude is very similar to the First Step of A.A., "We admitted we were powerless over alcohol — that our lives had become unmanageable." If we are alcoholics, we must admit to powerlessness over alcohol before we can begin recovering. Jesus is asking us to admit that we are powerless in the world of the spirit. "Spiritually helpless" is the meaning of being poor in spirit. We must be like helpless little children on this journey.

We begin our journey as we come from our mother's womb. On this journey there is no turning back. As we live our days on earth, we discover sooner or later that our physical lives are destined for decay and death. If we are to have the good life that leads us to the kingdom of heaven, Jesus' great wish for each of us, we must begin our spiritual journey. We are beginners on a new spiritual road. The first thing we must do on this journey is recognize our helplessness. Because we are poor in spirit we must take the first step.

Because nobody enjoys being helpless, this first step is difficult to take. But, unless we take it, our physical destiny is all that is left for us. We are given the choice of either accepting or rejecting God. We have a very important decision to make.

I learned to face my powerlessness from a chaplain when I was a patient in a mental hospital a few years ago. The chaplain said, "Whether you believe in the story of Adam and Eve or not, you should listen to what God said to them about eating from the tree of knowledge of good and evil. The reason God asked them not to eat of it was that the knowledge belonged to God. It was the knowledge that is 'above the line.' We should not try to appropriate God's knowledge. If we recognize that, we have freedom."

The chaplain used Hitler as an illustration of a person trying to be God, resulting in slavery and death. He looked into my troubled eyes and said, "Dick, I think you're trying to reach over the line. Let God's domain be God's domain." When I took that advice I began to get well.

When we do accept our spiritual helplessness, we are rewarded with a promise from Jesus: we shall inherit the kingdom of heaven, the greatest destination of all. Again and again in the Bible we are told this is our great reward. The amazing thing is that the reward is ours for simply recognizing our own spiritual helplessness and acknowledging our need for God. This is called grace, amazing grace!

What's it like being a spiritual beginner? Remember the first time you skied, or swam, or gave a speech? You were probably unsteady and unsure of yourself. I remember my first public speech. I was thankful for the dais in front of me, because my knees were actually knocking.

A.A.s understand the insecurity of the shaky alcoholic, the newcomer to the Program who is trying to stop drinking or using other drugs. A.A.s help the newcomer along with care and the compassion of those who have been there before. The system works well; those of us who have been through the problem help those who are trying to get through.

But, how does a spiritual beginner get help? We often hear, "Read the Bible," "Say your prayers," "Go to church," or "I know a minister you should talk to." Sometimes we hear, "Repent and have a personal relationship with Jesus." All of these statements are filled with good intentions, but what shaky spiritual beginners need most is to realize God loves them and they are loved by others.

Sometimes this assurance is hard for us to give each other, especially for those of us who have ever been part of a traditional church. We may think of religion as a "personal" matter. Perhaps because we are rather unsure and unsteady in our faith, we don't feel like talking about it to anyone else.

How *should* we grow in our spirituality? We can practice spirituality by listening and reading, and sharing with others what we see and hear. We can begin on the "gentle slopes." Prayer is a gentle slope. The Beatitudes are gentle; Jesus began with those. In the Bible, the Gospel of John and the Book of Psalms are easy for beginners to understand.

Another way to begin is to ask questions of others. Jesus' disciples asked all kinds of questions. Though Jesus sometimes appeared frustrated with the questions, He did answer them. Perhaps there is something about religion today that makes asking questions hard. Maybe we think of religion as too intellectual, but the simple sharing of questions and the answers we have helps us grow. Often not knowing the answers together helps us grow.

Sometimes the more religious we appear to become, the greater difficulty we have accepting our own spiritual poverty. Some of us think spiritual poverty is behind us, and through time we've gotten rich. We can learn from the program of Alcoholics Anonymous. If we are recovering alcoholics, we know that we will always be powerless over alcohol. Isn't that true with our spiritual situation also? Though we grow, we do remain in spiritual poverty. This is necessary for our relationship with God.

As we recognize our powerlessness, our poverty of spirit, and our need for God, amazingly we are told we will enter the kingdom of heaven. Does this mean we are born again? I believe we are. We are born into the new journey of Jesus, simply by recognizing that we are at the beginning. This beginning leads to a new life. We're turning away from our old physical lives, like we turn away from alcohol and other drugs if we are alcoholics. This act will lead us out of wilderness.

2

. . . to relate to ourselves honestly

Are We Running From Reality?

Jesus wants us to live an abundant life and shows us how, step by step. Discovering this step-by-step system of the Beatitudes has been a joy. We have already learned the way to relate to God, and we have been promised the kingdom of heaven; the great destination is ours. We are asked now to become honest with ourselves. Even though we're just shaky beginners, the next step Jesus asks us to take looks very dark and somber. We're told we are blessed if we mourn. The step which may be the most difficult to understand is the second beatitude.

If the Beatitudes have a progression to them, why is "Blessed are they that mourn, for they shall be comforted," the second step? Mourning is associated with the feelings of grief we have when we lose someone dear to us. If mourning accompanies death, why are we involved in mourning at this early stage? It would seem our mourning should come near the end of our step-by-step process.

There is reason to believe that Jesus is talking about more than the grief we feel over the death of loved ones when He says we are blessed if we mourn. In all the other beatitudes, Jesus speaks of the way we should live all throughout our earthly lives. Why would He, in this beatitude, speak of a one-time happening — physical death? The words spoken in the beatitudes are not about one-time happenings. They are a lifetime guide. If we were meant to mourn only when we have lost a loved one, the subject doesn't appear to belong with the rest of the Beatitudes. Mourning in this beatitude must mean more.

11

Mourning is *leaning into* the hurts of life instead of running from them. It makes sense that we do this after we understand our poverty of spirit. The first beatitude has shown us *we need God.* The second beatitude shows us *why* we need God.

We know there are both positive and negative sides to life. But negative qualities in ourselves are difficult to accept, because we don't like the idea of living with these tough realities forever. We'd rather not have to deal with our negative side at all. The truth sometimes seems too awful to face.

So many of us feel inadequate and unlovable. Most of those feelings are built on some of the things we learned about ourselves as children. To make up for those unacceptable feelings, many of us go through our lives continually trying to prove we are okay. This effort to prove ourselves usually doesn't satisfy our needs.

For example, we need to know we are loved, and if, as children, we didn't receive that love for some reason, we may feel permanently emotionally abandoned. By not receiving the love we needed, we suffered an emotional loss we cannot go back and recover.

We have a choice. We can either face reality and mourn this loss, or we can ignore it. Mourning a loss hurts, so too often we would rather ignore our pain, looking for distractions from reality. We may try to go through life pretending, but deep inside reality is haunting us. As long as we ignore reality, we cannot be set free from those haunting feelings of hurt and loss we carry with us. Until we accept our painful realities, we cannot be comforted. Our acceptance is a form of mourning.

I believe we experience our own personal hell during painful times of our lives when we feel no comfort. Jesus tells us that when we are in those places we need to face our pain, because it is *real.* We cannot run from pain. His promise is we *will* be comforted; we will not remain in hell. We may be in a place of helplessness, we may feel it is hopeless. Our sad feelings will be real, but there is an answer for us. It may take time, it may take other people, it may even take a miracle; but there will be comfort for us.

The personal hell many of us experience is deep depression. Depression is a dark state in which we feel like it will be this way forever. A depressed person believes there is no way out. Those who are deeply depressed draw away from those who are trying to comfort them. People experiencing depression descend to a place where emotions can no longer be felt, because the real feelings hurt too much and they cannot face the pain. They have retreated to a place where they will no longer feel any pain. It seems like a place of safety, but it is without comfort. It is a place of hell.

A less familiar example of a place without comfort is the manic state some people experience. People who suffer from a manic high believe they have unlimited power, the power of God. They feel in control, able to take care of themselves and others. The person who has this illness believes the high is natural, but in truth it is unreal, accompanied by a distorted self-image. There is no comfort in this place, because the manic person feels no need for comfort. This place is elevated above feelings, and although well-disguised, this is another kind of personal hell.

I've done my share of running away from reality, and I've experienced both these terrible states of mind. But the people who helped me asked me to stop my running and face the dragons no matter how ominous they appeared. As one doctor of psychology told me, "You can't fight them if they come from behind as well as you can fight them face-to-face." The insanity comes from running. The comfort comes from acceptance.

If the Beatitudes are a process to a good life, I believe Jesus is saying to us that in the beginning of the process, the second beatitude, we must accept the darkness of our own lives *to see the light.* He doesn't tell us it will be easy. In facing His own death, He asked that the cup He had to drink from be taken away. But He knew it wouldn't be taken away. What He is saying to us now is that when we swallow from our cup of reality, *there will be comfort.*

The Second Step of Alcoholics Anonymous states, "Came to believe that a Power greater than ourselves could restore us to sanity." If we are recovering alcoholics, we accepted in this Step that a Power greater than ourselves was the only way out of our personal hell. The alcoholic insanity could not be comforted, but honest acceptance of powerlessness can be.

A.A.s accept that they were living in insanity. The insanity was an escape from reality. Life is hard to handle at times for us. Many of us find ways of running away from our reality. If we haven't chosen alcohol or other drugs, perhaps we have used food, sex, or work — anything to keep our minds off the negative or unhappy parts of our lives. We avoid our feelings of ineptitude and smallness, our selfishness, or our insecurity. Many of us try to keep these things out of our heads any way we can, but escaping only enslaves us more.

My own personal experience of mourning as it relates to the Twelve Steps was the incredible blow I received when I realized I was, in fact, *not God.* I was living a delusional, immature, and very often insane life (Step One), and I *had* to make a decision to turn my life over to God, my Higher Power (Steps Two and Three). I grieved the loss of my old life. It was all I knew and it was crazy, but it was mine. There are many days I grieve the loss of my old self-indulgent life while I pursue righteousness. It's a constant battle. I must take the first three Steps often, several times a day, for my powerlessness over *life.*

If we are recovering in A.A., we know comfort comes from the acceptance of a Higher Power. A.A.s do not create the comfort for themselves alone. Recovering alcoholics need God and each other. Jesus makes a similar statement throughout the Beatitudes. The power for the promises of the Beatitudes comes from God.

In this second beatitude, we must also accept our mortality, the difficult reality many of us don't want to think about. Our denial of reality is our form of insanity. The tough reality is that our bodies die. Through the truth of sadness comes the truth of comfort. Jesus says *in death there is life.* Through our true mourning comes our acceptance. And with acceptance comes comfort. We can go ahead with our earthly lives after a loved one's death and know we will die too, but there will be another life for us. That is our comfort.

Jesus is saying we must turn and face the truth, making a choice to turn away from insanity. When we accept and feel reality, we walk into the comforting spirit of a loving God. Even though we are asked to mourn, it is the pathway to life.

3

*. . . to prepare ourselves to accept
the will of God*

Once You Get on the Diving Board,
It's Best to Go Into the Water

I like to use the dictionary. It makes clear what is unclear, straightening us out most of the time. But one word the dictionary doesn't define too well is the word meek. Webster says that *meek* means 1. patient and mild; not inclined to anger or resentment (I like that definition), 2. too submissive; spineless and spiritless (I don't like this one).

When Jesus said, "Blessed are the meek, for they shall inherit the earth," could He have meant the spineless and spiritless people? I doubt it. He could have meant the people who were patient and mild and not inclined to anger, but I don't believe this was His primary meaning of meek.

I believe Jesus got His definition of meek from the Old Testament use of the word. We should try our best to get the correct meaning of this important word to understand how meaningful the third beatitude is to us.

The Bible says, in Chapter 61 of Isaiah, "The spirit of the Lord is upon me; because the Lord has anointed me to preach good tidings unto the meek: He has sent me to bind up the brokenhearted, to proclaim liberty to the captives and the opening of the prison to them that are bound." In Isaiah, meek is connected to brokenness and need.

The 37th Psalm says, "Those that wait on the Lord shall inherit the earth." The psalm goes on, "But the meek shall inherit the earth and shall delight themselves in the abundance of peace." Here it seems that meekness and waiting on the Lord are synonymous.

In the first two steps of our step-by-step journey of the Beatitudes, we have gotten our relationships both with God and with ourselves in order. The next step is preparation for moving outward into relationships with others.

Now that we have begun to accept our spiritual poverty and the truth about ourselves, we realize we are meek and broken people in the sense of the Isaiah passage. We are like the psalm in that we are waiting on the Lord. Meekness in the Beatitudes means *waiting on the Lord*. Meekness is being available to God's will. Meekness is being like soft clay. Meekness is being ready and willing, and with God's help, able to do His work in the world, but broken and needing Him to make us whole. In the word "meek" is the reality of our smallness and the understanding that, without God, we will stay poor and broken.

Moses is the only person in the Bible who is actually described as meek. Moses was not a public speaker, but he was available to do the will of God. And so to this meek man, God said, "Now, therefore, go and I will be with your mouth and will teach you what you should say."

The Third Step of A.A. says, "Made a decision to turn our will and our lives over to the care of God *as we understood Him.*" This is very similar to the third beatitude. A recovering alcoholic has made this decision to turn self-will over to God's will. This is also what a meek person does — it's what Moses did — and what Jesus and Peter and Paul did. It is becoming available to the power of God.

How do we become available? One thing we can do is wait. A friend of mine once said that to be a Christian is to be like a tool of the carpenter. Maybe the carpenter doesn't need the tool right now; but he will need it, and the tool must be ready to do its job when called upon.

We don't like to wait. We feel useless when we wait. We wait for buses, other people, doctors, elevators, and it's boring. I don't think waiting for God is quite like that.

Waiting for God is preparing. The Bible prepares us. Prayer prepares us. Silent listening does too. But more important than all these are the attitudes we have when we wait. Are we hopeful? Are we expectant? Do we believe miracles can happen in our lives? *Yes* is the *meek* answer.

Another way to think about being meek is in "giving up." Giving up is almost un-American. But think of it this way. We have personal will. It can be egocentric, stubborn, and determined. In relationships those qualities, more often than not, separate us from others. The other side of those qualities is surrender. Instead of listening to self-will, we give ourselves up to God's will.

Many people draw away from this step because it sounds like life is going to be strict, no fun, and boring if we surrender our lives to God. We may have been made to feel that way by some religious people, but we shouldn't. We may have to listen to our inner values more than we used to, but Jesus isn't telling us to have a life without fun. He's trying to show us how life can be abundant.

The meek person says, "I'm not boss anymore." Standing in the way of our saying this is *pride*. Pride serves *me*. Meekness serves God. We get in the way of being our best selves, and so we have to get out of our own way. The part of us that wants to run the show and wants others to know how wonderful we are has to step out of the way so God's will can make us really wonderful.

This step of willingness is important for our personal excellence. It puts our energy into purposeful action and gives us a sense of direction. We begin to feel that direction move us, and we start to understand what Paul said: "In all things, God is working for good." When we accept our meekness, we begin to sense that we are a part of that good.

And what is our reward? The earth.

In the Old Testament, the reward literally was land. In the 37th Psalm, those who waited on God, the meek, were going to inherit this land. This was "The Promised Land." But Jesus' message had a new promise, the kingdom of heaven. Even though Jesus repeated the psalmist's statement about the meek inheriting the earth *word for word*, I believe there was something new in His promise.

What the meek inherit is the *responsibility* for the earth. We become available to God on this earth and become willing to serve His will on the earth. We become a part of God's hands, voice, and caring love on this earth. Acceptance of the promise carries responsibility. Responsibility is a part of our relationship with God. Along with our willingness to accept God's way for our lives comes the responsibility to Him, to ourselves, and now to the world around us. That is being meek.

I've sometimes thought of this step as the most exciting step, because of the commitment meekness demands. It's something like being on a diving board. Once you get up on a diving board, you're almost committed to diving or jumping into the pool. Jumping, though you may be filled with fear, is a natural conclusion to getting on the diving board.

We can back off. I did this once, when I was young, and I fell and hurt myself. The kids coming up the ladder of the diving board couldn't believe someone was trying to come back down. This wasn't the direction people usually go on a diving board. It was hard to back down the ladder and, in my embarrassment, I fell down the last part *and that hurt*. I left the pool feeling like I was still backing up. Fear beat me that time.

Being meek isn't the *act of diving* into a pool of relationships; it is *being ready and willing* to take that dive and that risk. And even though we don't know how it's going to be, we have faith and we are as ready as we can be for this new direction. Sometimes, as we climb up to the diving board, we feel meek in the way it was defined in the dictionary, especially if the board is high. Once we're there, afraid or not, most of us jump in. Knowing we will do this is being meek.

In our meekness, our willingness, our losses are fewer. There we glimpse the life God has in store for us. We don't see into the future, but we do feel a sense of God's will going out in front of us. Our lives are led in a single direction.

4

*. . . to accept, trust, and give our time
to righteous relationships in our lives*

The Fourth Step Is the Heart

Where are we after the first three beatitudes? We are finding ourselves spiritually helpless, trying to face our own reality, and becoming available to God's will for our lives. But what are we available for?

The answer is found in one word: relationships. Relationships are at the heart of the Bible; they are our reason for living. Jesus tells us the importance of relationships in the fourth beatitude, "Blessed are they which do hunger and thirst for righteousness for they shall be filled." What does righteousness have to do with relationships? Absolutely everything!

We must define "righteousness" first to get the real meaning out of this beatitude. Many of us think righteousness is another word for morality or doing the "right" thing. But that's not righteousness — not completely. There is the difficulty of deciding whose morality to adopt. Who decides which are high morals and which are low? This is all very confusing and too much like the judgmental Old Testament version of right and wrong, which was determined by the civil law at the time. Jesus brought us a completely new way of life with these beatitudes.

I believe we can best define righteousness in terms of how we fulfill our important relationships. Our righteousness can be seen as *satisfying the demands of our relationships.* Understanding this definition is important for us, because this is what so much of this journey is all about.

Sometimes we think our spiritual life is entirely separate from our relationships with ourselves and others. But, right relationships are what our spirituality is all about. Our relationship with God guides us into the right relationships with others.

The Beatitudes deal with a trinity of relationships and each has its own demands. Being righteous is satisfying those demands. The relationship trinity includes:

1. Our relationship with God
2. Our relationship with ourselves
3. Our relationships with others

Life is about these three kinds of relationships, and to emphasize this, Jesus stepped out of the rhythm of His beatitude poetry a bit to show us the need to "hunger and thirst" for good relationships. For our spiritual journey, our basic need for good relationships parallels our physical need for food and water to live. It's that important! But what are the demands of God we must satisfy to be righteous?

The Demands of God

The 31st Chapter of Jeremiah says, "I will put my law within them, and I will write it upon their hearts: and I will be their God, and they shall be my people." This is the Lord speaking through Jeremiah and it is a compact Old Testament statement about the human relationship with God. God made a promise to the human race connected to His demands in the form of laws. Man would fulfill those demands, and God would satisfy the people's need for land, freedom, and forgiveness. God demanded this relationship. God forgave the sins of people when they broke the law, even though breaking the law was not *righteous*.

Eventually the law became too arbitrary, and much like today's confusing morality, was determined primarily by man and not God. People fell away from the relationship with God, and He could not tolerate this lack of what should have been at the heart of their lives. The human relationship with God was dying, and He needed to do something.

So, God supplied the bridge for the relationship in the person of Jesus Christ. This new relationship is defined in the eighth chapter of John. Jesus says, "If you continue in My word, you are truly My disciples, and you will know the truth, and the truth will make you free. Truly, truly, I say to you, every one who commits a sin is a slave to sin. The slave does not continue in the house forever; the son continues forever. So if the Son makes you free, you will be free indeed."

The requirements for our relationship with God have been satisfied for us by Jesus. We now have a relationship with God. We did not have much to say about it; we were powerless. God has done the work. It is up to us to accept this.

I meet many people who, for one reason or another, don't believe in the concept of a loving personal God. Most of them have been turned off by the way religion was thrown at them and they rebel at official "this is how you must believe" religion. And so, they create a concept of God in the image they want. For many people, this is a necessity to have any faith in God at all, and sometimes it works.

What does not work in our lives is developing a spirituality that involves no desire on our part to do what God requires. If we give no thought to listening for God's will for our lives, we are trying to maintain control. When we insist on sitting in the driver's seat, we find we begin to develop problems.

Sometimes we think we are religious but we don't necessarily have a relationship with God. We do "religious" things, but we don't have spiritual relationships. According to the Bible, our relationship with God begins through the grace of God. God gives us the gift of His relationship with us. We have been given the best way to use that gift with the lessons for living we learn from the Beatitudes. In Twelve Step programs, this is called "working the Program." Working the Steps is the way to sobriety and serenity. Following the lessons Jesus taught is the way to spiritual fulfillment.

The Demands of Self

Do we really have relationships with ourselves? Yes. We think things over and decide our actions. We dress in clothes we like and wear our hair the way we want. We experiment with our lives. The person you have inner knowledge of is yourself. We know things we do not share with anyone else. Sometimes we wish those private things were not a part of us. In fact, we often come to hate ourselves for some of those inner truths and images we know so deeply and darkly.

But what demands should we make? The one demand above all others is that we be true to ourselves. Sometimes we want to run from our own realities — the parts of ourselves we simply do not want to accept. Those are the hard facts we need to face and mourn.

The second beatitude deals with the relationship we have with ourselves. As long as we face our large and small defects, we are being honest in this relationship. "To thine own self be true" is the one big relationship demand on us. Without it, we will have great difficulty moving on to other relationships.

The Demands of Others

There are demands that must be satisfied to create good relationships with others: to be honest and worthy of trust, to be accepting, and to give time to these relationships.

Without trust, a good relationship cannot even begin. The foundation of a relationship is honesty. Lies are enemies to righteousness. Dishonesty and falseness create unhappy and difficult relationships for us. Jesus had strong distaste for hypocrites, because they can't be truly close to others. Having trust is being able to believe and rely on another person.

Little children are trusting toward their parents. They rely on their parents to be there when needed. Children trust parents to supply all their needs. This is why Jesus asks us to be like little children in our faith. God supplies our needs. We can rely on that promise.

Without acceptance of others as they are, there can be no real relationship. If we don't base our relationships on the truth about ourselves and others, the false identities we've created cause insecurity and miscommunication. We simply need to accept each other for who we really are.

If we fail to devote time to our relationships, they fade out of our lives. We have to invest ourselves in the people we want relationships with.

We can see where we are in our relationships by looking at those people we trust and who trust us, those we have accepted and who have accepted us, and those to whom we devote our time. This is a simple test that lets us evaluate our relationships with others. We can also apply this test to our relationships with God and ourselves.

Another need in our relationships is obedience. Many of us don't like the idea of obedience. We rebel against it. This word has old associations for us and causes some of our emotions to stir. It may bring out our resentments against authority and religion. The demand for obedience may have caused more people to fall away from religion than anything else. Confusion may be the cause. Whom do we obey? Which rules are we to obey?

Obedience is as confusing as morality in this way. Many people disagree with rules and laws, and rebel rather than obey them. My minister told me an interesting fact. The root words for *obedience* mean to listen intently. I find it interesting that our society finds both listening and obedience difficult. In relationships, listening is important. Without really listening to each other, we can't communicate. If we could connect the meaning of obedience to listening, I think we'd develop better relationships.

We all have our own value systems. We each have our inner truths. Our truths and value systems make their own demands on us. Satisfying those requirements is another way we are righteous. Society's values do seem to change. But as long as we are obedient to and *listen* to our inner values, we

will live a righteous life. What would *total* righteousness be? I
believe it would be a life of *Trust, Obedience (listening),
Time,* and *Acceptance* with the people we *Love.*

The fourth beatitude leads us into righteous relationships.
And when we have those right relationships, what is the
promise to us?

We are told we will "be filled." But, filled with what? We
hear we have hungered and thirsted, and then we are filled.
Near the end of His life on earth, Jesus told us, "Whenever
two or three of you are gathered in My name, I will be
amongst you."

In the Old Testament, when the word "filled" is used, it is
often connected to the word "glory." The "glory filled the
room," or the tabernacle, or some other place. In the New
Testament, the word *filled* is associated with the *spirit.* We
are filled with the Holy Spirit. We began the journey poor in
spirit, and now we are filled with the spirit. Places used to be
"filled with glory," now people are filled with spirit. This is a
spiritual journey.

The Fourth Step of A.A. is "Made a searching and fearless
moral inventory of ourselves." In some ways the fearless
moral inventory is like the step of mourning. The goal is to
find the truth. And if we are recovering people in A.A., we
share what we have learned about ourselves in our moral
inventory with our Higher Power and another person in our
Fifth Step. Sharing our true selves in the Fifth Step is like a
step of righteousness. The goal is *truthful* relationships.

5

*. . . to accept our spiritual equality with all
people and to work toward equality in our
personal relationships*

The Mercy We Show Others
Will Come Back to Us

The story of the Good Samaritan has four characters. One
man lies beaten and helpless in a ditch by the side of the
road. Two men walking along the road passed by without
offering to help. A Samaritan does stop to help him. When
we hear or read that story from the Bible, most of us believe
we should identify with the helpful Good Samaritan and try
to be like him. That is right, we should.

However, if we identify ourselves with the man who
needed help, the man in the ditch, I believe we can understand what Jesus is asking us to do and why. Most of us, in
some way and at some time, have been in a "ditch" during
our lives and couldn't help ourselves. We may not have been
physically beaten, but we have been hurting. And perhaps
someone helped us. If we have come from a state of powerlessness and brokenness to a healing place, we know the
importance of our healers; we can understand the idea of
mercy more easily. We know from experience why it is
important to help others when they are helpless.

This is the heart of Alcoholics Anonymous. A person who
has been broken and hurt can feel empathy for another
hurting person. In A.A., alcoholics help other alcoholics.
That is *mercy*.

Mercy has a balancing effect — especially spiritual mercy.
And on this spiritual journey of the Beatitudes, Jesus says,

"Blessed are the merciful for they shall obtain mercy." This mercy we are asked to give others is the same mercy we need for ourselves. Our merciful acts come back to us. That which is given is returned to the giver. We are told that on this spiritual journey all people are equal. Our mercy for each other is shared by equals.

Some of us think we are being merciful when we help those who are less fortunate than we are. Yes, that is mercy, but we are usually thinking of people's material circumstances, not spiritual.

Now, I don't mean to imply that mercy of this kind is not real. It is, but thinking of mercy solely in a materialistic sense will not lead us to the mercy Jesus wants us to show. Remember, these beatitudes have to do with a new way of life, and our new lives are primarily involved with our spiritual way.

We admit to being poor in spirit. This is similar to the philosophy in the fellowship of A.A. Alcoholics all begin their recoveries by admitting to powerlessness over alcohol. There is equality in sharing the same predicament. And we are equal to each other in our poverty of spirit. In recognizing this equality and acting on it, we are merciful.

Another story in the Bible that teaches mercy is the story of the prodigal son. When that son returns home after spending all his inheritance, the father sees him coming up the road. The father doesn't wait at the house when he sees him; he runs down the road to his son, and hugs and kisses him. The father seeks the same level as his son. This is mercy — seeking to be on the same level with others, to love them, and to share equally. Yes, the mercy we show others is the mercy we need for ourselves.

Mercy is simply an act of helping our fellow human beings discover that they are not alone, they are not separated, they are a part of our lives. We're all in the same spiritual boat. But so many people do feel alone, especially when they are afraid. If they can share their fear with us and feel our efforts to understand them, they will experience mercy and so will we — especially if we share some of our own fear with them.

People feel alone when they have lost a loved one. We may not be able to feel their grief, but we can try to give them loving support. That is mercy.

People feel so alone when they are guilty and remorseful. We know how this feels, so we share our feelings with them to lessen their loneliness.

The Fifth Step of Alcoholics Anonymous — "Admitted to God, to ourselves, and to another human being the exact nature of our wrongs" — may help us understand this concept of mercy.

How could this act demonstrate mercy? It sounds more like a need for mercy than a demonstration of giving mercy. Where does mercy begin? Could it begin when we begin to admit the exact nature of *our* wrongs? I think so, because an act of true confession is meeting our fellow human beings on an equal basis. In confessions we start to understand and relate to another, perhaps saying, "There but for the grace of God go I."

On the other hand, when we're so busy trying to prove to our fellow travelers what good people we are, where is there room for mercy to grow? What we may be doing is trying to justify ourselves. If, by our good acts, we're worrying about impressing those around us, we create separation between us. This is not an act of mercy.

If we open ourselves to relationships with the intention of sharing and serving, then we have opened ourselves to being merciful and, at the same time, to *receiving mercy* from others.

One of the two founders of A.A. spoke about how much religion had helped him in his life, yet he felt it had not really shown him how to stay sober. He said, "I couldn't understand what was wrong. I had done all the things that those good people had told me to do . . . attend meetings, read the Good Book, go to church and pray. I had done them, I thought, very faithfully and sincerely. And still I continued to get

31

drunk regularly. But the one thing that they hadn't told me was the one thing that worked . . . attempt to help someone."

This is the Golden Rule. If we have been told of one best way to treat others, it is usually a form of "Do unto others what you would have them do unto you." From the Lord's Prayer we learn, "Forgive us our sins as we forgive those who sin against us." Our mercy returns to us.

And so we come down from our mountaintops and share our fears and insecurities, and as we confess the truth, mercy for us begins. But it is even more than this. Having mercy also means sharing our riches. "For I was thirsty and you gave me drink, I was hungry and you gave me food, I was a stranger and you welcomed me, I was naked and you clothed me, I was sick and you visited me, I was in prison and you came to me. Truly I say to you, as you did it to one of the least of these my brothers, you did it to me."

We have inherited the earth. The way to begin that responsibility is with mercy toward others. Jesus has made a change in us. He directs our loving acts away from sacrifices to God and toward charity to others. This beatitude is a new commandment to love our neighbor as we love ourselves. The sacrifice to God that was such a large part of the Old Testament is exchanged by Jesus into a merciful people-to-people relationship.

Scholars of the Bible have described mercy using many words: sympathy, love, compassion, pity, graciousness, steadfast love, brotherly or motherly feelings, and forgiveness.

Mercy can be all of those qualities, but the best description I know is "a loving act." If love is wanting the best for another person then mercy is the *act* of doing the best for another person. Mercy takes action. And we'll know when we've been merciful, because others will be merciful toward us too. Mercy has a reciprocal effect.

Earlier in our journey, we were promised to be filled. Though we are filled with the Holy Spirit, we are still poor in spirit. How can this be? It is similar to "an alcoholic always being an alcoholic." The recovering alcoholic is always just one drink away from a drunk. The follower of Jesus is on a step-by-step pathway to abundant living. What would Jesus followers' "one drink away" be? I believe it is spiritual pride. If we don't continually accept our spiritual poverty, then our spiritual pride will get in our way and lead us into acting like little gods, incapable of true mercy.

So, by the grace of God, we are filled with spirit at the same time we are poor in spirit. When we know and accept this, we can be truly merciful.

6

. . . to listen to God for guidance

The Rest Stop That Becomes a Battlefield

We find it possible to accept our poverty of spirit, along with mourning, meekness, righteous relationships, and our need to show mercy. When we stop and think, all these are within the realm of possibility. With God's help, these qualities are all attainable goals.

If we wish to go deeper into our relationships, God has provided a way. That deeper way is provided in the final three beatitudes. In the next beatitude we learn about our purity of heart. "Blessed are the pure in heart for they shall see God."

To be pure in heart — now that just doesn't sound possible. We know our hearts are not "pure." How do we gain purity of heart? Looking carefully at the words of Jesus, we will learn what we can do. Our hearts and our purity seem to be connected to our eyes and ears. In the thirteenth chapter of Matthew, Jesus explains, "To you has been given to know the secrets of the Kingdom of Heaven, but to them it has not been given. For to him who has, more will be given and he will have abundance; but from him who has not, even what he has will be taken away. This is why I speak to them in parables, because *seeing* they do not *see* and *hearing* they do not *hear*, nor do they *understand*."

Prophesied by Isaiah was, "You shall indeed *hear*, but never understand, and you shall indeed *see* but never perceive, for this people's *heart* has grown dull and their *ears* are heavy of hearing and their *eyes* have closed lest they should perceive with their *eyes* and hear with their *ears* and understand with their *heart* and turn for me to heal them. But blessed are your *eyes* for they see and your *ears* for they hear."

We have been told these two senses are conduits to our heart and our inner knowledge. Therefore, we can help create a pure and impure heart depending on how we use our perception.

We live in a noisy, busy world and if we simply see and hear the outside world, our purity of heart will be difficult to find. Most of our outside world doesn't offer us much motivation to become pure of heart. But is Jesus asking us only to look and listen to this world? I don't think so.

This is our rest stop on this journey of the Beatitudes. It is a time to draw away from the noise and crowds of the world and find our own places of quiet with God.

So many of us get caught up in being "do-gooders." We think we can prove to God that we are wonderful people and deserving of front-row attention in the Kingdom of God. Some of His disciples felt that way. "Look at me, Jesus. Look at all I'm doing. See how busy I am." The purification step will help us avoid this trap.

What Jesus asks us to do in this step is stop, look, and listen — to really listen. It is a time of quiet. But what should we look and listen for? And how will it make our hearts more pure?

Once again, let's look at the Twelve Steps of Alcoholics Anonymous. The Eleventh Step says, "Sought through prayer and meditation to improve our conscious contact with God *as we understood Him*, praying only for knowledge of His will for us and the power to carry that out." This Step seems to be a purity of heart step too. It shows us the need for silent communication with God.

The Sixth Step of A.A. is: "Were entirely ready to have God remove all these defects of character." God does in this Step. He removes our defects, but we must be *entirely ready*. Just as we did when we became meek, we place ourselves in a position to become pure. But what is this position? There are ways we can become available to God for purification of our hearts: we take a position of silence, a position of detachment from the world's control, and we become undivided and whole again.

Silence

Thomas Merton, the writer and contemplative, believed that all the activities in the life of a monk were directed at being pure of heart. He thought of it as total commitment to God and complete acceptance of ourselves and our situation as willed by God. Purity of heart, to Merton, meant giving up deluded images of ourselves and exaggerated estimates of our own capabilities.

Purity of heart is connected to new self-identity, an enlightened awareness of our true selves. Merton believed the way to this awareness was through meditation and contemplation. Seeking God was seeking the full understanding of His will in our lives.

Would we have to be monks to seek this self-understanding? No. We simply place ourselves in the position of silence and let God do His work. Then we must be willing to accept the truth. "Know thyself" becomes the goal of meditation. Our false images, the character defects, must be given up so we can be free to be real.

Many of us have problems with silence. What should we be listening for? Does God really speak to us? I believe God's direction comes through our contemplation, if we will shut out the noise of the world. Silent meditation is another way of waiting for God. In our meekness we became available to God. In our silent trust, we can become pure in heart. In the silence of looking and listening to God, He asks us for our undivided attention.

Wholeness

There is in each of us a *real* person and that true identity is our best. We often bury this identity under who we think we *should* be, based on what the rest of the world thinks. We become divided, a combination of our real and our false identities. We really get in our own way. In our step of purity, Jesus asks us to let God remove our defects.

We must be willing to accept our true identities and be willing to give up all the shoulds. We can then be whole.

How do we know what is false? Look for things that create fear in us, our need to impress others, and every "should." But when we are true to our values, we are being our real and our ideal selves.

Detachment From the World's Control

As long as we listen to the world to see who we should impress, we will be blind to understanding God's will for our lives. If we seek our approval from the world, we cannot find purity of heart.

Jesus called the devil the father of lies. The world presents false images for us to desire. In a real sense, our lives are battlefields and the war is fought over control of our hearts. Who or what will have control over our lives? Will we, the world, or God? Will alcohol or drugs control us? Will we choose our own pride or our Higher Power? Whose values will control our actions? We need to answer these questions here in our step of purity.

In the speech he prepared for the acceptance of his Nobel Peace Prize, Alexander Solzhenitsyn said the responsibility of the artist in the world was "One Word of Truth" amidst a world of lies. The lie will not win on this battlefield if we stand up with *one word of truth.*

Righteousness, as we have learned, is satisfying the demands of our relationships. And in this purity step, God has some demands. He demands our eyes, ears, and hearts. The world demands the same from us. And Jesus tells us we cannot serve two masters. This is our step of silence and rest, but it is also our step of commitment. There is a battle going on.

But haven't we already been promised the kingdom of heaven? We also have the promise of comfort, mercy, and the

Holy Spirit. Wouldn't that mean the battle is over and Jesus has won? Yes, but we need to be careful not to turn control back over to our self-will or our pride.

We can see God in our lives and in the lives of others. But proudly assuming the authority of God abuses our close relationship with Him. It was the prideful, "know-it-all" religious person that angered Jesus most. We need our purity of heart step to keep us humble and truthful with ourselves, not inflated with our "greatness."

7

. . . to risk making peace where peace is needed

Peacemaking Is Dangerous Business

In the seventh beatitude, Jesus tells us, "Blessed are the peacemakers for they shall be called the children of God." Being a child of God seems very peaceful. And if that is so, why is it dangerous?

What is peacemaking? I believe it is making relationships right. In this context, peacemaking has to do with more than just our personal relationships. This beatitude involves peacemaking for those outside of our own personal circles; this is what makes peacemaking so dangerous. Many of us voice words of wanting peace, but true peacemakers, those who take action for peace are few and far between. Peacemaking demands more than most of us are willing to give.

My Aunt Alice was a peacemaker. She became involved in helping make peace in relationships outside of her own personal sphere. In the early 1930s, she helped develop the first family court in Milwaukee, Wisconsin. Couples wanting a divorce had to go through my Aunt Alice to have their cases heard by a judge. She was well-known as "The Woman Who Saved 10,000 Marriages."

How do we become peacemakers? Let's take a simple example — making peace with those who have given us a hard time. There has been a falling out or a separation, and we have been hurt. Probably the other person was hurt too. Peace will not be made by sweeping all those feelings under the carpet and trying to forget.

What does it take to make peace with that person? Peace is usually made by some form of admission. That first step of approaching the other person takes effort. It seems so hard. Sometimes we'd rather forget it, but if we do, the chance for reconciliation is gone. That we may have harmed someone is something most of us don't like to admit.

People in Twelve Step programs deal with peacemaking in the Eighth and Ninth Steps: "Made a list of all persons we had harmed, and became willing to make amends to them all." and "Made direct amends to such people whenever possible, except when to do so would injure them or others."

I asked Aunt Alice how she did her peacemaking with all those people wanting divorces. She said in the first talk with the couple a lot of blaming usually went on. Then she would talk privately with each of them. If, in these private talks, she discovered a concern for each other, a truth that didn't come out in the first talk, she would bring the couple back together and ask each of them to share what they had told her in the private talks. Often these people would be reluctant, but when the truth came out, the couple had a place to begin again. It may have been the only remaining ember, but even this was something. This was the beginning of the making of amends — reconciliation.

This kind of peacemaking feels risky. It feels like we're giving away too much of ourselves without getting anything back. We don't like to admit we were wrong, because it hurts. Yes, it is painful at first, but then the truth sets us free.

The goal of a recovering alcoholic is serenity. If we are recovering, we have found serenity in the admission of our powerlessness and our need for God or our Higher Power. That is tough enough for some of us, but it's even tougher to make the specific admissions of the things we have done to harm others. As peacemakers, and for our serenity, we must do this.

True peacemakers see the needs for peace outside their immediate personal lives. The goal of the peacemaker is the same as the righteousness seeker: to make relationships right, even if they are not personal ones.

Jesus did this. Mahatma Gandhi and Martin Luther King did this, too. They believed strongly enough in something to devote their lives to making changes. All three of these men were killed for their beliefs. Peacemaking can be dangerous! Many people don't like the interference of peacemakers.

To be peacemakers in this world, we need — as Jesus, King, and Gandhi needed — strong faith and strong convictions about the importance of peace. Through the first six beatitudes, our faith should have the foundation and spiritual security we would need in our attempts to be peacemakers. Without this strength, our peacemaking efforts would be quickly eroded by the strong efforts of the world's angry voices telling us to mind our own business.

When true peacemakers begin showing us the truth, fear often makes us deny what they are telling us. Think about Jesus and Gandhi and King. Think about the lights they tried to shine on their troubled worlds. Think of the necessary changes their truth revealed. Think of what the world did to them for their efforts.

Peacemaking doesn't always involve such great efforts as those three men made, but we can all be peacemakers. Even smaller efforts at peace usually involve risk. We might get involved in the marital separation of close friends, helping a co-worker who has been treated unfairly, intervening in a child abuse situation, or helping a lonely elderly person.

Picture coming into one of these situations with all good intentions. How would we be received? Some would welcome our peaceful motives, but there might be those who would greatly dislike our involvement. How would we know whether our help was going to be accepted? How would we know whether to stay involved and work for peace or to stay away? Peacemakers must continually examine their motives.

Which comes first, peace within ourselves or peace with others? Can we have one without the other? Can we have inner peace without first having peace with God?

Jesus says, "I have made you well, go in peace." A famous benediction ends, "The Lord lift up His countenance and give you peace." And in Luke, the angels say, "Glory to God in the highest and peace to His people on earth." So, like faith, peace is a gift from God — a blessing.

The step we take toward peace comes after we have let God bring us purity of heart. The inner enemy of peace is fear. And the journey we've taken so far is meant to strengthen our faith to the point of making us able to experience peace within. Faith becomes the power we need to move out and become peacemakers in the world. But if faith is our power, understanding is our way.

When those couples my aunt spoke to began dealing with the truth, it was probably hard. But then they began to understand each other. The light started shining in those ten thousand marriages when they began to understand.

When understanding is impossible, serenity can come through giving up our need to understand. A.A.s use the Serenity Prayer:

> *God, grant me the serenity*
> *To accept the things I cannot change,*
> *Courage to change the things I can,*
> *And wisdom to know the difference.*

It is a way to peace and serenity.

In the Gospel of John, Jesus, in His farewell to His disciples, concludes by saying, "I have said this to you, that in Me you may have peace. In the world you have tribulation; but be of good cheer, I have overcome the world." Jesus also said, "Greater things than I do, you will do."

If we think of His words as directives to be peacemakers, we see that we are to mirror the ways of Jesus. In spite of what happens to many peacemakers on the battleground, He has given us His assurance that He has won, and along with Him, we will win.

8

. . . to accept the consequences of our beliefs

For Theirs Is the Kingdom of Heaven

"**B**lessed are they which are persecuted for righteousness'
sake, for theirs is the kingdom of heaven." This is the
last of the eight beatitudes, the conclusion of a journey
beginning with poverty and seeming to end in persecution. To
understand this final statement, we must look at two important facts.

First, we have to keep in mind that this beatitude does not
encourage us to *seek* persecution; instead, it merely shows
Jesus' awareness that those who live a righteous life might, at
times, be persecuted because of that righteousness.

Second, we should again acquaint ourselves with the
concept of righteousness — *righteousness is satisfying the
demands of a relationship.* Chapter Four discussed the relationship trinity, that threefold interdependency between our
relationships with God, ourselves, and others. Each has
demands — and these are rigid demands — which must be
met in order to keep the relationship healthy and strong. The
relationships that we maintain with ourselves and others are
gradually evolving, and they depend upon our communication with others and our honesty with ourselves. The last of
this trinity — our relationship with God — is God-given, not
man-made. God's grace established this relationship; therefore, we can maintain this gift only by our receptiveness to
and acceptance of it.

What does persecution for righteousness' sake mean? The
religious persecution that happens to outspoken priests in
Poland, or to the missionaries attempting to build churches

in the hills of Nicaragua, may not happen to us. But, on the basis of our being righteous when we fulfill the demands of our relationships, we may be in a position to be hurt. Trying to do the will of God, as best we understand it, and being hurt in the effort, would be persecution for righteousness' sake. This does happen to us sometimes. Many of us have been hurt by those we have trusted. Many of us have been hurt for standing up for our values and beliefs. Some of us have taken risks in our relationships and been disappointed. Perhaps we do not have outer scars because of our righteous efforts, but many of us suffer inner pain and persecution.

As we look at the concept of being persecuted for our righteousness, many of us think we are not involved. And perhaps that is true. But most of us feel persecuted by something! Many of us are running, afraid, or hurt. We may feel persecuted by life. Rather than being persecuted for righteousness' sake, we may be persecuting ourselves by running from righteousness.

It may begin when we search for our comfort or fulfillment in alcohol, drugs, sex, and material things. At first, it may feel like a haven from our feelings of not being loved, a place we can lose ourselves. Eventually, these things become painful sources of persecution for us.

This is pain that the Beatitudes and the Twelve Steps of A.A. can free us from. People who are happy and secure, like those in Twelve Step programs and those who are accepting of their spirituality, do not choose to be persecuted. But it happens, and when it does, it is often the result of the righteous practice of the overriding principles of that Program or that faith.

The last Step of Alcoholics Anonymous is: "Having had a spiritual awakening as the result of these Steps, we tried to carry this message to alcoholics, and to practice these principles in all our affairs." Correspondingly, in the Beatitudes, Jesus tells us how to carry His message to others by practicing "righteous principles." We may be persecuted by others who do not believe as we do, but we are willing to accept the consequences of our beliefs because of the promises that have been made to us.

THE PROMISES

The eighth beatitude has promised us the kingdom of heaven. This is the same reward we were promised for recognizing our poverty of spirit, or our powerlessness. I am convinced it is a cycle, and that this last beatitude leads us once again to the first. We are powerless over our suffering, so we let go of it and turn it over to our Higher Power.

This cycle tells us the wonderful truth about God's love for us. Jesus has said if we recognize that we are powerless and God is all-powerful, He will grant us all that He has: the kingdom of heaven. We don't have to do anything more than this for this great reward.

This message is different. In most of our daily living, we are used to earning what we have. We might wonder why, if we can have the kingdom of heaven just for recognizing we are helpless, we need to follow a set of guidelines. But, what an abundant life on earth we will find if we use the Beatitudes as our plan for living!

Like the Twelve Steps of Alcoholics Anonymous, the Beatitudes are our way to the good life. They give us direction, and they guide us to our highest good. We have the promises of Jesus.

The first beatitude . . .	to relate to God through our powerlessness
The second beatitude . . .	to relate to ourselves honestly
The third beatitude . . .	to prepare ourselves to accept the will of God
The fourth beatitude . . .	to accept, trust, and give our time to righteous relationships in our lives

The fifth beatitude . . .	to accept our spiritual equality with all people and to work toward equality in our personal relationships
The sixth beatitude . . .	to listen to God for guidance
The seventh beatitude . . .	to risk making peace where peace is needed
The eighth beatitude . . .	to accept the consequences of our beliefs
The first promise:	The kingdom of heaven
The second promise:	Comfort
The third promise:	Responsibility for the earth
The fourth promise:	The Holy Spirit
The fifth promise:	Mercy
The sixth promise:	God's vision of the world around us
The seventh promise:	To be like Jesus
The eighth promise:	The kingdom of heaven

THE TWELVE STEPS OF ALCOHOLICS ANONYMOUS*

1. We admitted we were powerless over alcohol — that our lives had become unmanageable.
2. Came to believe that a Power greater than ourselves could restore us to sanity.
3. Made a decision to turn our will and our lives over to the care of God *as we understood Him.*
4. Made a searching and fearless moral inventory of ourselves.
5. Admitted to God, to ourselves, and to another human being the exact nature of our wrongs.
6. Were entirely ready to have God remove all these defects of character.
7. Humbly asked Him to remove our shortcomings.
8. Made a list of all persons we had harmed and became willing to make amends to them all.
9. Made direct amends to such people wherever possible, except when to do so would injure them or others.
10. Continued to take personal inventory and when we were wrong promptly admitted it.
11. Sought through prayer and meditation to improve our conscious contact with God *as we understood Him,* praying only for knowledge of His will for us and the power to carry that out.
12. Having had a spiritual awakening as the result of these steps, we tried to carry this message to alcoholics, and to practice these principles in all our affairs.

---

*The Twelve Steps are taken from *Alcoholics Anonymous*, published by A.A. World Services, New York, NY, pp. 59-60. Reprinted with permission.

Hazelden

Conscious Contact
Partnership with a Higher Power
  by Gail N.
  There is a Power greater than ourselves. It is something we can experience, something we can feel. A practical, inspiring look at spiritual experience, this pamphlet describes alternative perceptions of a Higher Power, and explains how our chosen perception can be enriched by others, nature, and even ourselves. By pinpointing our favorite forms of resistance, *Conscious Contact* reveals many ways to improve our contact with God, as we understand God. (24 pp.)
Order No. 5250B

Not-God
A History of Alcoholics Anonymous
  by Ernest Kurtz, Ph.D.
  The most complete history of A.A. ever written, *Not-God* contains anecdotes and excerpts from the diaries, correspondence, and occasional memoirs of A.A.'s early figures. A fascinating and authoritative account of the discovery and development of the program and fellowship that we know of today as Alcoholics Anonymous. (363 pp.)
Order No. 1036A

The 12 Steps to Happiness
A Handbook for All 12 Steppers
One Man's Interpretation
  by Joe Klaas
  This very popular book explores each of the Twelve Steps as they relate to all recovery programs. A truly fresh approach that unlocks the crystal clear mystery of the Twelve Steps. (78 pp.)
Order No. 1053A

For price and order information, please call one of our Customer Service Representatives.

Pleasant Valley Road
Box 176
Center City, MN 55012-0176

(800) 328-9000
(Toll Free. U.S. Only)
(800) 257-0070
(Toll Free. MN Only)
(800) 328-0500
(Toll Free. Film and Video Orders. U.S. Only)
(612) 257-4010
(Alaska and Outside U.S.)